RHODE ISLAND

RHODE ISLAND

A Scenic Discovery

Photographed by Steve Dunwell

Introduction and text by Roger Vaughan

Produced by Foremost Publishers, Inc.

To Dorothy June

Rhode Island is a certain environment, a specific place, the nation's smallest state, a state greatly reduced in land mass by the ocean's intrusion. This is a book about Rhode Island the place — its color, shape and texture.

It is a gorgeous place in all seasons. In spring the subtle shades of wild flowers and blooming bushes roll across fields. Daffodils and forsythia crowd the highways. The ocean breeze meanders the wide rivers and bays to temper summer's heat. In the fall, Indian summer is long and seductive, a fantasy of warm days followed by nights crisp enough for bundling.

Winter turns fields the color of cornbread crust slashed with the dark streaks of stone walls and patched with snow. Under the gray skies and dark clouds of winter storms, and against the slate hues of rivers, ponds and ocean, the spent, bleached-out fields glow with a reassuring warmth that can resist the deepest frost. In the lowlands, giant dried grasses with tassels of fluff sway with the wind and catch fire from the setting sun.

All seasons share the sudden fog — an intriguing visitor — which arrives in great wet clumps and hides us, temporarily, from even our neighbors.

In its isolation of timeless, natural elements, *Rhode Island* is a nostalgic book. Even people, when they appear, are reduced to archetypal symbols. Many scenes are photographed in ways the Indians must have known them. They evoke a strong response, poignant visions of earliest beginnings and ancestral doings. The identification is keen. Words like "heritage" come to mind. Nostalgia's worth lies in both its comforting properties (the past is, after all, safe), and the lessons it might afford. Nostalgia is a touchstone for the formation of values.

Rhode Island is a romantic book, a personal vision. And yet even as an idealistic view there is no fantasy involved. Every photograph in the book was taken in 1975. Hence the theme of discovery: many of these are not familiar images.

The vision for *Rhode Island* is that of Jim Patrick of Foremost Publishers Inc., who has lived in the state all his life. He collaborated with Steve Dunwell, whose assignment was to photograph that vision. Dunwell approached the job with journalistic thoroughness: first with research, including an Audubon Society list of areas recommended for preservation, then by driving 8,000 miles around the state in eight months, shooting, as it turned out, a photograph per mile.

The result is a visual adventure for even the most knowledgeable and long-term resident of the state. The book reveals Rhode Island as a mysterious place full of surprises. South Sea Island pools are hidden behind thick clumps of bayberry and wild rose; down a wooded, untrodden path, a familiar ocean view becomes a startling new vista; houses with stark, mid-western Gothic flavor peer upon the sea from the green hills of Block Island; egrets nest on desolate islands of rock; and always there is the shoreline, 384 miles of flat beaches, snug harbors and hidden coves, open bays and hostile rocky promontories.

Rhode Island transcends time to present a photographic celebration of the physical entity. It is at once a look at yesterday, today, and tomorrow — a statement of where we are. The reaction to it must be, in the visitor's vernacular, "You got a nice place here." We do indeed.

Roger Vaughan

In December

December's grim gray hand has touched the sea
That seems to mock in anger at the sky
Brooding above in gray immensity,
While o'er the water scores of gray gulls fly.

And as one looks out on this scene of gray
He finds no beauty of which he would boast,
Until the breaking waves fling showers of spray
Against the sea wall on this storm-swept coast.

George Franklin Merritt

11. Spindrift flies off breaking waves during stiff blow at Newport's Brenton Point.

12. Rocks at Mohegan Bluffs, Block Island, bask at low tide like bearded ancients.

13. Gulls scan for leftovers as crew of dragger Lucy M tends gear in Block Island Sound.

14. Serene amid the lavish, turn of the century glow at Newport's Marble House, a cellist prepares for a concert.

15. Dusted with new snow, evergreens in a Newport formal garden spill between statuary like a waterfall.

16. A Galilee fishing boat motors into the dawn to begin her day.

17. Arctic hues of a winter sunset color the tide pools at Price Neck, Newport.

18. Between tides, seaweed covered rocks along Newport coast wear a crusty coat of new snow.

19. Mussels in profusion, and scattered periwinkles coexist in bed of Jamestown kelp.

20. A relic of the past, this Jamestown windmill still counts sunsets.

21. A final touch is applied to a carefully plaited mane before judgement in the show ring at Little Compton.

22. Two hundred year old lichens cling to weathered stones in burying ground, Little Compton Commons.

23. The steeple of the First Congregational Church in Little Compton is a classic Rhode Island sentry.

24. Pleased at a job completed, a Galilee fisherman waits in a trawler's hold to send up his last basket.

25. Old lobster pot buoys, identification tags of the sea, brighten up a shed in Little Compton.

26. Full and on the rise, the moon is trapped momentarily in the arch of a Newport Bridge tower.

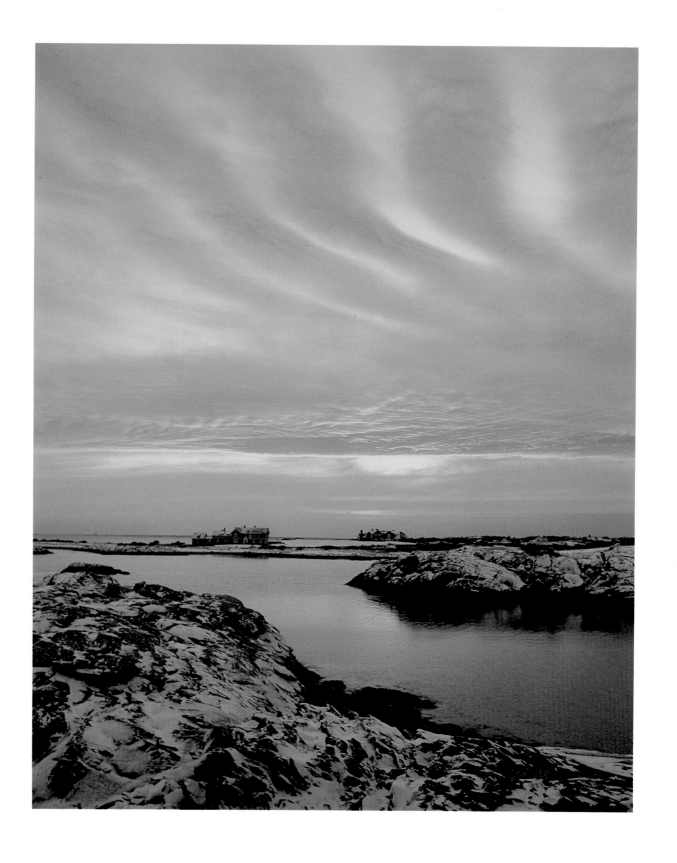

Mist

All I can see of sea or land
Is each single wave on the strip of sand
As it breaks in white, and then slips away,
Lost in thick-folded veils of gray.

All I can know of the heights of sky
Is the call of the plovers as they fly
Above the low-hung fog, unseen;
Shrill cries, far-falling, clear and keen.

Yet the sense of a measureless depth and height
Is more surely felt than when skies are bright
And the blue sea-levels shift and shine
Till they touch the wide horizon's line.

Augustus Mendon Lord

31. The reservoir at Slatersville steams in the heat of early morning summer sun.

32. Oblivious to snow and cold, fishermen intently plumb the depths of Olney Pond, Lincoln.

33. A clump of meadow evergreens braces against blowing snow.

34. With spring still a hope away, this Shannock farmer turns over last year's corn stubble to make room for potatoes.

35. Weathered barn siding, Plain Meeting House Road, West Greenwich.

36. Squeezed beneath the shape of a looming work boat hull, a Tiverton boat builder sands the heavy keel timber.

37. While gulls hover and scream like hungry airborne cats, whiting fishermen bend to their task.

38. Flowing softly as a maiden's hair, a waterfall in Scituate cascades the rocky steps.

39. A flourishing tree in Glocester testifies to the virtue of sinking roots in rock crevices.

40. Barn and man in Greene, R.I. have aged well, and together.

41. Every spring, a barn in Hope, R.I., sits atop a mound of dandelions.

42. Early morning dew.

43. Undisturbed by a boy's chores, a calf dozes in the milking parlor of a dairy farm in Shannock.

44. The tidal pools off Beavertail's shore are underwater gardens alive with creatures.

45. Beavertail Light, looking southwest along the eastern shore.

46. West shore, Beavertail.

September

                            . . . groves and woods,
Checker'd by one night's frost with various hues,
While yet no wind has swept a leaf away,
Shine doubly rich.

Carlos Wilcox

51. The crescent moon hangs between two landmark towers on the East Side of Providence.

52. Polished beach stones pause on a desert of windblown sand—State Beach, Block Island.

53. Smooth hulled racing yachts skid like leaves across a sea of rare tranquility as racing begins off Block Island.

54. The East Side of Providence is history, tradition, and polished brass door knockers.

55. Old, red brick houses and enchanting, cobbled courtyards lurk among the lanes of the East Side.

56. Summer is flying headlong into a quarry pool in Lincoln.

57. Rhododendron blossoms, Ministerial Road, South Kingstown.

58. The lobsterman's world is often a solitary, suspended sort of place.

59. The grand mansions of Newport's Ocean Drive shrink beside stormy seas.

60. The millpond overflow at Usquepaug glows with ethereal phosphorescence.

61. Wildflowers, Chepachet.

62. Old, wood frame houses of the East Side contrast with new additions to the Providence skyline.

63. Benefit, street of many colors, rich in history and restorations.

64. A woodlot on Woonsocket Hill goes to color in early fall.

65. In South Tiverton, a small community clings to a thin peninsula between tidal marshes and the Sakonnet River.

66. Under foreboding skies, a winter storm attacks Newport with the roar of surf and acres of white foam.

The Snow Storm

Announced by all the trumpets of the sky,
Arrives the snow, and, driving o'er the fields,
Seems nowhere to alight: the whited air
Hides hills and woods, the river, and the heaven,
And veils the farm-house at the garden's end .

Ralph Waldo Emerson

71. Atop the State House dome, The Independent Man defies rain and storm and dark of night.

72. Autumn's biggest show-offs are maple leaves.

73. Treasures from bygone years surround antique shop owner on Franklin Street, Newport.

74. With fork and basket, one can still dig a meal of quahaugs from beneath the rocky beach at Bristol.

75. Seagull tracks along Mount Hope Bay near Bristol.

76. Dinghies bob patiently off the yacht club dock at Sakonnet Point as summer fog delays the games.

77. Respite.

78. Black-eyed Susans.

79. It is a fact that no one has ever written a song about the Kingston railroad station.

80. A common egret takes flight with classic grace from a nest on Tiverton's Gould Island.

81. On idyllic summer days, Briggs Beach, Little Compton, inspires dreaming.

82. Goldenrod (bless you).

83. A statue in the misty dawn, a horse receives the first warmth of the sun.

84. Shelf of a general store in Hope Valley.

85. Bent to his work, a blacksmith at the state fair in East Greenwich fits a heavy customer.

86. Wickford Harbor in hibernation.

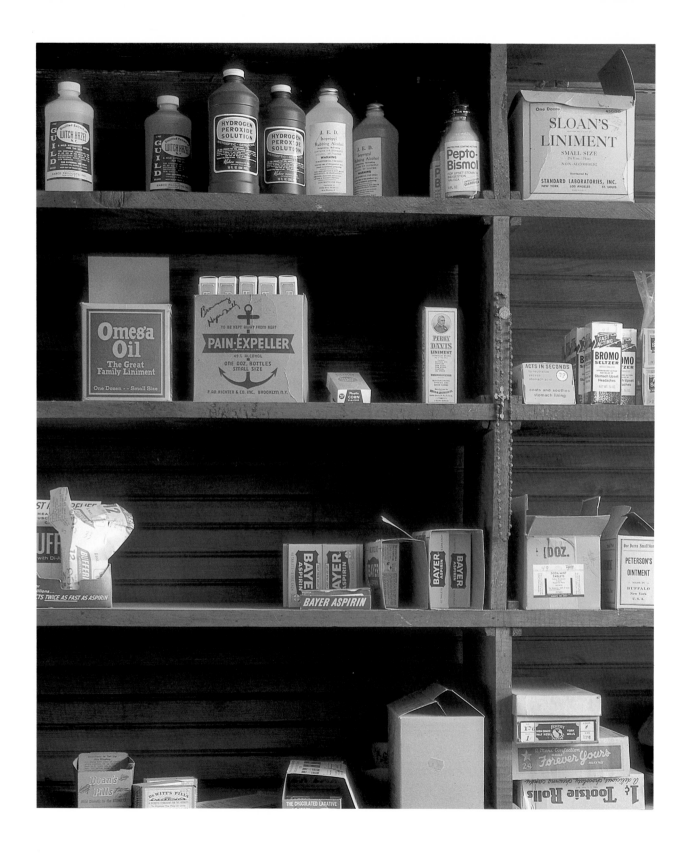

Open Ocean

The placid sun of autumn shines, —
    The hurrying knell marks no decline,
    The rush of waves, the war of brine,
Force all, and grandeur, in thy lines.

Could the lone sand-bird once enjoy
    Some mossy dell, some rippling brooks,
    The fruitful scent of orchard nooks,
The loved retreat of maid or boy!

William Ellery Channing

91. The hard working ocean battlements of Newport's famed Cliff Walk.

92. Summer fern profusion, rooted in the damp, thick and sweet.

93. Frost killed ferns, brown and brittle, taking final flights.

94. The sun sets over frothy tide pools at Warren Point, Little Compton.

95. Brenton Point, Newport.

96. Magnolia blossoms.

97. Serious business at the candy counter, general store, Chepachet.

98. Polished by the sea, bleached by the sun, beach rocks rest on Block Island at low tide.

99. Second Beach, Newport, overlooked by the tower of St. George's School.

100. Tiverton pastoral: Sin and Flesh Brook.

101. Set in motion by flowing grasses beneath the water, young boys are drawn by the magic of the Blackstone River at Ashton.

102. Happy with a load of sweet corn at Shannock.

103. Detail of a barn door in Gazzaville.

104. Enjoying a simple pleasure in Shannock.

105. Little Compton Commons, looking southwest from the air, is nestled in trees and painted green.

106. The barnacle encrusted rocks of Haffenreffer Point, Bristol.

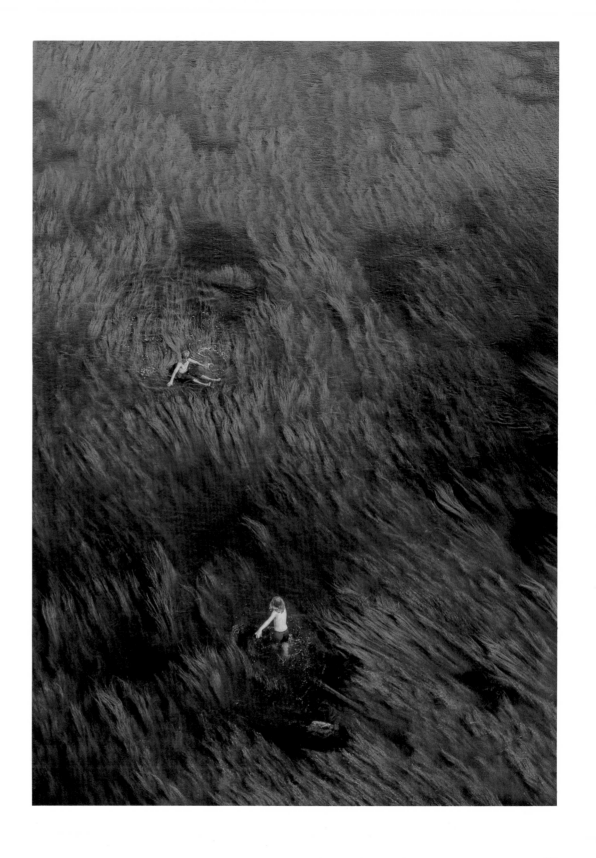

In Hardwood Groves

The same leaves over and over again!
They fall from giving shade above,
To make one texture of faded brown
And fit the earth like a leather glove.

Before the leaves can mount again
To fill the trees with another shade,
They must go down past things coming up.
They must go down into the dark decayed.

They *must* be pierced by flowers and put
Beneath the feet of dancing flowers.
However it is in some other world
I know that this is the way in ours.

Robert Frost

111. Harbor lights burn against the brilliant afterglow of a late spring day at New Harbor, Block Island.

112. Block Island houses perch on green, rolling hills.

113. Solitary sunbathing beneath Mohegan Bluffs, Block Island.

114. Potted flowers on the whitewashed doorstep of a house in Old Harbor, Block Island.

115. Inside this Block Island summer house, the rocking chair waits.

116. Sakonnet lobstermen talking business.

117. The fishing shack of H.N. Wilcox & Co. at Sakonnet Point is more than a place to stow gear.

118. Brenton Tower, on far horizon, warns vessels of deadly Brenton Reef, off Newport.